# THE
# TRUTH
# ABOUT
# LOVE

ABRAMS NOTERIE, NEW YORK

CONTENTS

You have to love. You have to feel.
It is the reason you are here on earth.

You are here to risk your heart.
You are here to be swallowed up.

And when it happens that you are broken, or
betrayed, or left, or hurt, or death brushes near,
let yourself sit by an apple tree and listen to the
apples falling all around you in heaps, wasting
their sweetness. Tell yourself you tasted as many
as you could.

LOUISE
ERDRICH

Love has always been my job.

In my early-to-mid twenties, I was a singer-songwriter who wrote and performed love songs all over the world. I spent many hours sitting at a piano, or with a guitar in hand, working to say something brilliant and incisive and unique about love in a three-minute song. Had I found a book of quotes about love to refer to during this time, I would have brought it to every writing session, certain that inspiration was only a few pages away.

Eventually, I made the transition from writing songs to writing novels. For the past fifteen years, every day that I sit down to write, I ask myself the same questions about the heroines and heroes in my books: Why are they afraid to love—and what will it take for them to no longer be scared so that they can finally embrace it? It is my job as a novelist to mine the deepest darkness, and to seek out the brightest beauty, in not only my character's hearts and minds, but also in the world around them. And at the heart of every one of my books is an unshakeable belief in true love and its magnificent power, even when the path to love is sometimes rocky and difficult. The reason is simple— love is far more than just a job for me.

Love is waking up beside my husband every morning to get the kids ready for school and then falling exhausted into bed beside him every night after homework is done and the dinner dishes are washed and put away. Love is cheering my kids on at a soccer game on a Saturday afternoon and then struggling later that same day with how to best talk with them about difficult subjects such as war, loss, heartbreak. Love is supporting, and being supported by, my extended family and friends in good times and bad. Love is seeing my dog running over, tail wagging, with hope in his eyes that it's time for a walk, and then loving him just as much even after finding out that he's gotten into the garbage (again!).

The true magic of love for me—whether as a mom, wife, daughter, sister, friend, or writer—is that it's the most universal language of all. Countless generations in every country, in every language throughout history have been compelled to write about love . . . and I can't imagine we'll ever stop wanting to pour out our hearts onto the page as we try to figure out just what it is about love that always has, and always will, make our hearts skip a beat.

—*Bella Andre, New York Times* bestselling author of the Sullivans series

Once upon a time there was a boy
who loved a girl, and her laughter was
a question he wanted to spend his
whole life answering.

NICOLE KRAUSS

IF YOU ARE NOT
TOO LONG, I WILL
WAIT HERE FOR YOU
ALL MY LIFE.

*Oscar Wilde*

When I saw you I fell
in love, and you smiled
because you knew.

*Arrigo Boito*

I'm saying that I'm
a moody, insecure,
narrow-minded, jealous,
borderline homicidal bitch,
and I want you to promise
me that you're okay with
that, because it's who I am,
and you're what I need.

*Jeaniene Frost*

THERE IS A MADNESS
IN LOVING YOU, A
LACK OF REASON
THAT MAKES IT FEEL
SO FLAWLESS.

*Leo Christopher*

IT'S HARD TO RESIST
A BAD BOY WHO'S A
GOOD MAN.

*Nora Roberts*

The decision to kiss for
the first time is the most
crucial in any love story. It
changes the relationship
of two people much more
strongly than even the final
surrender, because this kiss
already has within it that
surrender.

*Emil Ludwig*

I DON'T KNOW
HOW TO KISS,
OR I WOULD KISS
YOU. WHERE DO
THE NOSES GO?

*Ernest Hemingway*

. . . . I was beginning to believe that a very few times in your life, if you were lucky, you might meet someone who was exactly right for you. Not because he was perfect, or because you were, but because your combined flaws were arranged in a way that allowed two separate beings to hinge together.

LISA KLEYPAS

How did it happen that their lips
came together? How does it happen that
birds sing, that snow melts, that the rose
unfolds, that the dawn whitens behind
the stark shapes of trees on the quivering
summit of the hill?

VICTOR HUGO

SOUL MEETS SOUL
ON LOVER'S LIPS.

*Percy Bysshe Shelly*

How delicious
is the winning
of a kiss at
love's beginning.

*Thomas Campbell*

A kiss is strange. It's
a living thing, a
communication, a whole
wild emotion expressed in
a simple moist touch.

*Mickey Spillane*

KISSING IS A
PLEASANT
REMINDER THAT
TWO HEADS
ARE BETTER
THAN ONE.

*Rex Prouty*

I cannot fix on the hour,
or the spot, or the look, or
the words, which laid the
foundation. It is too long
ago. I was in the middle
before I know that
I had begun.

*Jane Austen*

I ne're was struck before
that hour with love so
sudden and so sweet.
Her face, it bloomed like
a sweet flower and stole
my heart away complete.

*John Clare*

WHEN LOVE COMES
IT COMES WITHOUT
EFFORT, LIKE PERFECT
WEATHER.

*Helen Yglesias*

I could not tell you if I loved you the first moment I saw you, or if it was the second or third or fourth. But I remember the first moment I looked at you walking toward me and realized that somehow the rest of the world seemed to vanish when I was with you.

CASSANDRA CLARE

He felt now that he was
not simply close to her, but
that he did not know where
he ended and she began.

*Leo Tolstoy*

There is never a time
or place for true love.
It happens accidentally,
in a heartbeat, in a single
flashing, throbbing
moment.

*Sarah Dessen*

I LOOK AT YOU
AND SEE THE REST
OF MY LIFE IN FRONT
OF MY EYES.

*Unknown*

. . . a fire. But whether it is going to warm your hearth or burn down your house, you can never tell.

*Joan Crawford*

. . . an irresistible desire to be irresistibly desired.

*Robert Frost*

. . . something sent from heaven to worry the hell out of you.

*Dolly Parton*

. . . unpredictable and it's frustrating and it's tragic and it's beautiful. And even though there's no way to feel like I'm an expert at it, it's worth writing songs about—more than anything else I've ever experienced in my life.

*Taylor Swift*

KISS: A THING OF NO
USE TO ONE, BUT
PRIZED BY TWO.

*Robert Zwickey*

Love at the lips was touch
As sweet as I could bear;
And once that seemed too
much; I lived on air.

*Robert Frost*

I'M OXYGEN AND HE'S
DYING TO BREATHE.

*Tahereh Mafi*

Daisy, Daisy, give me your answer, do!
I'm half crazy, all for the love of you!
It won't be a stylish marriage,
I can't afford a carriage,
But you'll look sweet upon the seat
Of a bicycle built for two.

HARRY DACRE,
*Daisy Bell*

WE DON'T BELIEVE
IN RHEUMATISM AND
TRUE LOVE UNTIL
AFTER THE FIRST
ATTACK.

*Marie von Ebner-Eschbach*

The trouble with some
women is that they get all
excited about nothing—
and then marry him.

*Cher*

True love comes quietly,
without banners or flashing
lights. If you hear bells, get
your ears checked.

*Erich Segal*

I wished for nothing
beyond her smile, and to
walk with her thus, hand in
hand, along a sun-warmed,
flower-bordered path.

*André Gide*

ONCE IN A WHILE,
RIGHT IN THE MIDDLE
OF AN ORDINARY
LIFE, LOVE GIVES US
A FAIRY TALE.

*Unknown*

It's one thing to fall
in love. It's another to feel
someone else fall in love
with you and to feel a
responsibility toward
that love.

*David Levithan*

Millions and millions of years would still not give me half enough time to describe that tiny instant of all eternity when you put your arms around me and I put my arms around you.

JACQUES PRÉVERT

For it was not into
my ear you whispered,
but into my heart. It was
not my lips you kissed,
but my soul.

JUDY GARLAND

. . . then I did the simplest
thing in the world.
I leaned down . . . and
kissed him. And the world
cracked open.

*Agnes de Mille*

YOU KNOW YOU'RE
IN LOVE WHEN YOU
CAN'T FALL ASLEEP
BECAUSE REALITY IS
FINALLY BETTER THAN
YOUR DREAMS.

*Dr. Seuss*

TO BE FULLY SEEN
BY SOMEBODY, THEN,
AND BE LOVED
ANYHOW—THIS IS A
HUMAN OFFERING
THAT CAN BORDER
ON MIRACULOUS.

*Elizabeth Gilbert*

I realized I was thinking
of you, and I began to
wonder how long you'd
been on my mind. Then
it occurred to me: Since I
met you, you've never left.

*Unknown*

YOU HAVE
BEWITCHED ME
BODY AND SOUL,
AND I LOVE, I LOVE,
I LOVE YOU.

JANE AUSTEN

"To douchebags!" he said, gesturing to Brad.
"And to girls that break your heart,"
he bowed his head to me.
His eyes lost focus.
"And to the absolute fucking horror of
losing your best friend because you were
stupid enough to fall in love with her."

JAMIE MCGUIRE,
*Beautiful Disaster*

MAN IS THE
ONLY ANIMAL
THAT BLUSHES.
OR NEEDS TO.

*Mark Twain*

No matter how
lovesick a woman is,
she shouldn't take the first
pill that comes along.

*Joyce Brothers*

The magic of first love
is our ignorance that it
can ever end.

*Benjamin Disraeli*

WE ARE ALL
MORTAL UNTIL
THE FIRST KISS
AND THE SECOND
GLASS OF WINE.

*Eduardo Galeano*

. . . being stupid together.

*Paul Valery*

. . . an act of endless forgiveness, a
tender look which becomes a habit.

*Peter Ustinov*

. . . like war: easy to begin but very
hard to stop.

*H. L. Mencken*

. . . an untamed force. When we try to
control it, it destroys us. When we try
to imprison it, it enslaves us. When we
try to understand it, it leaves us feeling
lost and confused.

*Paulo Coelho*

. . . a canvas furnished by Nature and
embroidered by imagination.

*Voltaire*

Some things
are just perfect,
even when
they don't make
any sense.

BELLA ANDRE

What I want is to be needed.
What I need is to be indispensable to
somebody. Who I need is somebody
that will eat up all my free time,
my ego, my attention. Somebody
addicted to me. A mutual addiction.

CHUCK
PALAHNIUK

# #1 HIT SONGS ABOUT LOVE

You Always Hurt the One You Love
*Mills Brothers*

•

Love Me Tender
*Elvis Presley*

•

Will You Love Me Tomorrow
*The Shirelles*

•

I Can't Stop Loving You
*Ray Charles*

•

All You Need Is Love
*The Beatles*

•

Stop! In the Name of Love
*The Supremes*

•

When a Man Loves a Woman
*Percy Sledge*

Crazy Little Thing Called Love
*Queen*

•

I Want to Know What Love Is
*Foreigner*

•

The Power of Love
*Huey Lewis and The News*

•

What's Love Got to Do With It
*Tina Turner*

•

Crazy in Love
*Beyoncé*

•

I Will Always Love You
*Whitney Houston*

•

Love Will Find a Way
*Yes*

I fell in love with her courage, her sincerity, and her flaming self-respect. And it's these things I'd believe in, even if the whole world indulged in wild suspicions that she wasn't all she should be. I love her and it is the beginning of everything.

F. SCOTT FITZGERALD, on his wife, Zelda

BEING IN LOVE

If I knew that today would be the last time I'd see you, I would hug you tight and pray the Lord be the keeper of your soul. If I knew that this would be the last time you'd pass through this door, I'd embrace you, kiss you, and call you back for one more. If I knew that this would be the last time I would hear your voice, I'd take hold of each word to be able to hear it over and over again. If I knew this is the last time I see you, I'd tell you I love you, and would not assume foolishly you know it already.

GABRIEL
GARCÍA
MÁRQUEZ

I swear I couldn't love
you more than I do right
now, and yet I know
I will tomorrow.

*Leo Christopher*

They say when you are
missing someone that they
are probably feeling the
same, but I don't think
it's possible for you to miss
me as much as I'm missing
you right now.

*Edna St. Vincent Millay*

MY BOUNTY IS AS
BOUNDLESS
AS THE SEA,
MY LOVE AS DEEP.
*William Shakespeare*

O, my Luve is like a red, red rose,

That's newly sprung in June.

O, my Luve is like the melodie,

That's sweetly played in tune.

ROBERT BURNS

I love you not only for what you are,
but for what I am when I am with you.

I love you not only for what you
have made of yourself, but for

what you are making of me.

I love you for the part of me
that you bring out.

ELIZABETH
BARRETT
BROWNING

I'm here. I love you. I don't care if you
need to stay up crying all night long,
I will stay with you. There's nothing you
can ever do to lose my love. I will protect
you until you die, and after your death I
will still protect you. I am stronger than
depression and I am braver than loneliness
and nothing will ever exhaust me.

ELIZABETH
GILBERT

Doubt thou the stars are fire;

Doubt that the sun doth move;

Doubt truth to be a liar;

But never doubt I love.

WILLIAM
SHAKESPEARE

YOU PIERCE MY SOUL.
I AM HALF AGONY,
HALF HOPE . . . I HAVE
LOVED NONE
BUT YOU.

*Jane Austen*

In your light,
I learn how to love.
In your beauty,
how to make poems.
You dance inside my chest
where no one sees you.

*Rumi*

Perhaps it is our
imperfections that make us
so perfect for one another.

*Douglas McGrath*

I WANT TO DO
WITH YOU WHAT
SPRING DOES WITH
THE CHERRY TREES.

*Pablo Neruda*

This is the true measure
of love; when we believe
that we alone can love, that
no one could ever have
loved so before us, and that
no one will ever love in the
same way after us.

*Johann Wolfgang
von Goethe*

Have you ever been in
love? Horrible isn't it?
It makes you so vulnerable.
It opens your chest and it
opens up your heart and
it means that someone
can get inside you and
mess you up.

*Neil Gaiman*

It's not the face, but the
expressions on it. It's not
the voice, but what you say.
It's not how you look in that
body, but the thing you do
with it. You are beautiful.

*Stephenie Meyer*

. . . WE KISS, AND IT
FEELS LIKE WE HAVE
JUST SHRUGGED OFF
THE WORLD.

*Jim Shahin*

My true-love hath my
heart, and I have his,
By just exchange one
for the other given:
I hold his dear, and mine
he cannot miss,
There never was a better
bargain driven.

*Sir Philip Sidney*

Ask the child why it is born;
ask the flower why
it blossoms ask the sun why
it shines. I love you because
I must love you.

*George Upton*

. . . composed of a single soul
inhabiting two bodies.

*Aristotle*

. . . friendship that has caught fire.
It is quiet understanding, mutual
confidence, sharing and forgiving.
It is loyalty through good and bad
times. It settles for less than perfection
and makes allowances for human
weaknesses.

*Ann Landers*

. . . that condition in which the
happiness of another person is
essential to your own.

*Robert A. Heinlein*

. . . a friendship set to music.

*Joseph Campbell*

. . . not the dying moan of a distant
violin—it's the triumphant twang of
a bedspring.

*S. J. Perelman*

The greatest happiness
of life is the conviction that
we are loved; loved for
ourselves, or rather, loved
in spite of ourselves.

VICTOR HUGO

Love is patient, love is kind.

It does not envy, it does not boast,
it is not proud.

It is not rude, it is not self-seeking, it is not
easily angered, it keeps no record of wrongs.

Love does not delight in evil but
rejoices with the truth.

It always protects, always trusts,
always hopes, always perseveres.

*THE BIBLE*,
1 Corinthians
13:4-8

I loved her against reason,
against promise, against
peace, against hope,
against happiness, against
all discouragement
that could be.

*Charles Dickens*

You are the answer to every
prayer I've offered. You are
a song, a dream, a whisper,
and I don't know how I
could have lived without
you for as long as I have.

*Nicholas Sparks*

I AM IN YOU AND
YOU IN ME, MUTUAL
IN DIVINE LOVE.

*William Blake*

I love you—I am at rest with
you—I have come home.

*Dorothy L. Sayers*

ONE LOVE, ONE
HEART, ONE DESTINY.

*Bob Marley*

IF YOU REMEMBER
ME, THEN I DON'T
CARE IF EVERYONE
ELSE FORGETS.

*Haruki Murakami*

How do I love thee?
Let me count the ways.
I love thee to the depth
and breadth and height
My soul can reach.

*Elizabeth Barrett Browning*

ONE OF THE
HARDEST THINGS
IN LIFE IS HAVING
WORDS IN YOUR
HEART THAT YOU
CAN'T UTTER.

*James Earl Jones*

Sometimes your nearness
takes my breath away and
all the things I want to say
can find no voice. Then, in
silence, I can only hope my
eyes will speak my heart.

*Robert Sexton*

The most important
things are the hardest to
say, because words
diminish them.

*Stephen King*

IF I LOVED YOU LESS,
I MIGHT BE ABLE TO
TALK ABOUT IT MORE.

*Jane Austen*

I LOVE YOU MORE
THAN I HAVE EVER
FOUND A WAY
TO SAY TO YOU.

*Ben Folds*

They invented hugs to let
people know you love them
without saying anything.

*Bil Keane*

Love is an endless mystery,
For it has nothing else
to explain it.

*Rabindranath Tagore*

. . . the way a drowning man loves air.
And it would destroy me to have you
just a little.

*Rae Carson*

. . . as certain dark things are to be
loved,
in secret, between the shadow and
the soul.

*Pablo Neruda*

. . . because the entire universe
conspired to help me find you.

*Paulo Coelho*

. . . like a fat kid loves cake!

*Scott Adams*

And this maiden she lived
with no other thought

Than to love and be
loved by me.

EDGAR
ALLAN POE
"Annabel Lee"

I love you without knowing how, or when, or from where. I love you simply, without problems or pride. I love you in this way because I do not know any other way of loving but this, in which there is no I or you, so intimate that your hand upon my chest is my hand, so intimate that when I fall asleep your eyes close.

PABLO NERUDA

YOU'RE NOTHING
SHORT OF MY
EVERYTHING.

*Ralph Block*

THOU ART TO ME A
DELICIOUS TORMENT.

*Ralph Waldo Emerson*

What I feel for you
seems less of earth and
more of a cloudless heaven.

*Victor Hugo*

If you live to be a hundred,
I want to live to be a
hundred minus one day
so I never have to live
without you.

*A. A. Milne*

There's this place in me
where your fingerprints still
rest, your kisses still linger,
and your whispers softly
echo. It's the place where
a part of you will forever
be a part of me.

*Gretchen Kemp*

IF I HAD A FLOWER
FOR EVERY TIME I
THOUGHT OF YOU. . .
I COULD WALK
THROUGH MY
GARDEN FOREVER.

*Alfred Tennyson*

BECAUSE I COULD
WATCH YOU FOR A
SINGLE MINUTE AND
FIND A THOUSAND
THINGS THAT I LOVE
ABOUT YOU.

*Unknown*

He does something to me,
that boy. Every time.
It's his only detriment.
He steps on my heart.
He makes me cry.

*Markus Zusak*

When someone loves
you, the way they talk
about you is different. You
feel safe and comfortable.

*Jess C. Scott*

HE'S MORE
MYSELF THAN I AM.
WHATEVER OUR
SOULS ARE MADE OF,
HIS AND MINE ARE
THE SAME.

*Emily Brontë*

I would like to be the air
that inhabits you for a
moment only. I would like
to be that unnoticed and
that necessary.

*Margaret Atwood*

For you see, each day
I love you more. Today
more than yesterday and
less than tomorrow.

*Rosemonde Gérard*

PROMISE ME
YOU'LL NEVER
FORGET ME BECAUSE
IF I THOUGHT
YOU WOULD, I'D
NEVER LEAVE.

*A. A. Milne*

I love thee, I love but thee
With a love that shall not die
Till the sun grows cold
And the stars grow old.

WILLIAM
SHAKESPEARE

Time was passing like a hand waving
from a train I wanted to be on. I hope
you never have to think about anything
as much as I think about you.

JONATHAN
SAFRAN FOER

. . . what happens to men and women
who don't know each other.

*Somerset Maugham*

. . . like the wind, you can't see it but
you can feel it.

*Nicholas Sparks*

. . . our true destiny. We do not find the
meaning of life by ourselves alone—we
find it with another.

*Thomas Merton*

. . . the silent saying and saying of a
single name.

*Mignon McLaughlin*

. . . putting up with someone's bad
qualities because they somehow
complete you.

*Sarah Dessen*

TRUE LOVE BEGINS
WHEN NOTHING
IS LOOKED FOR
IN RETURN.

*Antoine de Saint-Exupéry*

Thinking of you keeps me
awake. Dreaming of you
keeps me asleep. Being
with you keeps me alive.

*Unknown*

I love thee to the depth
and breadth and height
my soul can reach.

*Elizabeth Barrett Browning*

I hope you know that every time I tell you to
get home safe, stay warm, have a good day,
or sleep well what I am really saying is
I love you. I love you so damn much that it
is starting to steal other words' meanings.

UNKNOWN

To love at all is to be vulnerable. Love anything and your heart will be wrung and possibly broken. If you want to make sure of keeping it intact you must give it to no one, not even an animal. Wrap it carefully round with hobbies and little luxuries; avoid all entanglements. Lock it up safe in the casket or coffin of your selfishness. But in that casket, safe, dark, motionless, airless, it will change. It will not be broken; it will become unbreakable, impenetrable, irredeemable. To love is to be vulnerable.

C.S. LEWIS

ADVICE ON LOVE

Everyone, at some point in their lives, wakes up in the middle of the night with the feeling that they are all alone in the world, and that nobody loves them now and that nobody will ever love them, and that they will never have a decent night's sleep again and will spend their lives wandering blearily around a loveless landscape, hoping desperately that their circumstances will improve, but suspecting, in their heart of hearts, that they will remain unloved forever. The best thing to do in these circumstances is to wake somebody else up, so that they can feel this way, too.

LEMONY SNICKET, *Horseradish*

I love the way you smile
at me. I love the way your
hands reach out and hold
me near. I believe this is
heaven to no one else
but me.

*Sarah McLachlan*

I WOULD RATHER
SPEND ONE LIFETIME
WITH YOU, THAN
FACE ALL THE AGES
OF THIS WORLD
ALONE.

*J.R.R. Tolkien*

LOOK AFTER MY
HEART—I'VE LEFT IT
WITH YOU.

*Stephenie Meyer*

**FOREVER IS
COMPOSED OF NOWS.**

*Emily Dickinson*

Money can buy you a fine
dog, but only love can
make him wag his tail.

*Kinky Friedman*

I wish I could
turn back the clock.
I'd find you sooner
and love you longer.

*Unknown*

I need to see my own beauty and to continue to be reminded that I am enough, that I am worthy of love without effort, that I am beautiful, that the texture of my hair and that the shape of my curves, the size of my lips, the color of my skin, and the feelings that I have are all worthy and okay.

TRACEE
ELLIS ROSS

And remember,
as it was written, to love
another person is to see
the face of God.

*Victor Hugo*

WHERE THERE
IS GREAT LOVE,
THERE ARE ALWAYS
MIRACLES.

*Willa Cather*

LOVE CONQUERS ALL.

*Virgil*

For small creatures such
as we, the vastness is
bearable only through love.

*Carl Sagan*

For every beauty, there is an eye
somewhere to see it.

For every truth, there is an ear
somewhere to hear it.

For every love, there is a heart
somewhere to receive it.

IVAN PANIN

It does not matter what
you do in the bedroom
as long as you do not
do it in the street and
frighten the horses.

*Mrs. Patrick Campbell*

WHEN ANGRY,
COUNT TO TEN
BEFORE YOU SPEAK;
IF VERY ANGRY, A
HUNDRED.

*Thomas Jefferson*

HONESTY HAS RUINED
MORE MARRIAGES
THAN INFIDELITY.

*Charles McCabe*

Sex is a conversation
carried out by other means.
If you get on well out
of bed, half the problems
of bed are solved.

*Peter Ustinov*

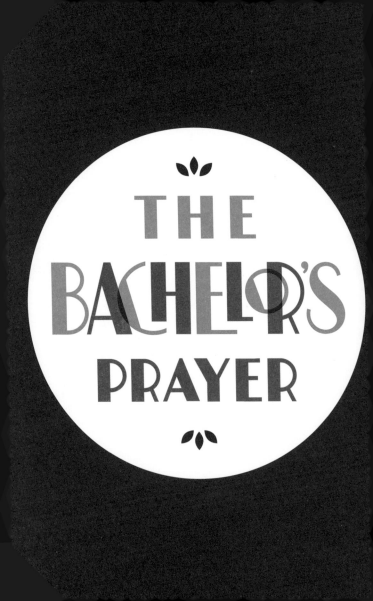

# THE BACHELOR'S PRAYER

I pray that I may not be married

But if I am to be married

that I may not be cuckold

but that if I am to be a cuckold

that I may not know it

but if I know it

that I may not care.

UNKNOWN

The beginning of love is to let those we love be perfectly themselves, and not to twist them to fit our own image. Otherwise we love only the reflection of ourselves we find in them.

*Thomas Merton*

LOVE ME WHEN I LEAST DESERVE IT, BECAUSE THAT'S WHEN I REALLY NEED IT.

*Swedish proverb*

DON'T SETTLE FOR A RELATIONSHIP THAT WON'T LET YOU BE YOURSELF.

*Oprah Winfrey*

Love does not consist of gazing at each other, but in looking outward together in the same direction.

*Antoine de Saint-Exupéry*

I BELIEVE IN LONG,
SLOW, DEEP, SOFT,
WET KISSES THAT LAST
FOR THREE DAYS.

*Kevin Costner
in* Bull Durham

Four sweet lips, two
pure souls, and one
undying affection—
these are love's pretty
ingredients for a kiss.

*Christian Nestell Bovee*

My child, if you finally
decide to let a man kiss
you, put your whole heart
and soul into it. No man
likes to kiss a rock.

*Lady Chesterfield*

KISSES MAY NOT
SPREAD GERMS, BUT
THEY CERTAINLY
LOWER RESISTANCE.

*Louise Ericson*

A career is a wonderful thing, but you can't snuggle up to it on a cold night.

MARILYN
MONROE

I think men who have a
pierced ear are better
prepared for marriage.
They've experienced pain
and bought jewelry.

*Rita Rudner*

NEVER FORGET
THE NINE MOST
IMPORTANT WORDS
OF ANY MARRIAGE:
I love you.
You are beautiful.
Please
forgive me.

*H. Jackson Brown Jr.*

IT'S NOT WHAT
YOU LOOK AT
THAT MATTERS, IT'S
WHAT YOU SEE.

*Henry David Thoreau*

DO NOT SEEK THE
BECAUSE—IN LOVE
THERE IS NO BECAUSE,
NO REASON, NO
EXPLANATION, NO
SOLUTIONS.

*Anaïs Nin*

The best and most
beautiful things in this
world cannot be seen or
even heard, but must be
felt with the heart.

*Helen Keller*

Love is not only
something you feel,
it is something you do.

*David Wilkerson*

LOVE CANNOT SAVE
LIFE FROM DEATH;
BUT IT CAN FULFILL
LIFE'S PURPOSE.

*Arnold Toynbee*

OF ALL FORMS OF
CAUTION, CAUTION
IN LOVE IS PERHAPS
THE MOST FATAL TO
TRUE HAPPINESS.

*Bertrand Russell*

There is no disguise which
can hide love for long
where it exists, or simulate
it where it does not.

*François de La Rochefoucauld*

In a great romance, each
person plays a part the
other really likes.

*Elizabeth Ashley*

Feeling too much
is a hell of a lot better
than feeling nothing.

NORA
ROBERTS

Take each other for better
or worse, but not
for granted.

ARLENE DAHL

Love endures only when
the lovers love many things
together and not merely
each other.

*Walter Lippmann*

If you believe yourself
unfortunate, because you
have loved and lost, perish
the thought. One who
has loved truly, can never
lose entirely.

*Napoleon Hill*

THE HUMAN HEART,
AT WHATEVER AGE,
OPENS ONLY TO THE
HEART THAT OPENS
IN RETURN.

*Maria Edgeworth*

Tis better to have
loved and lost

Than never to have
loved at all.

ALFRED
TENNYSON

. . . sharing your popcorn.

*Charles Schulz*

. . . a letter on pink stationery.

*Charles Schulz*

THERE IS NO REMEDY
FOR LOVE BUT TO
LOVE MORE.

*Henry David Thoreau*

The course of true love
never did run smooth.

*William Shakespeare*

LIPS THAT TASTE
OF TEARS, THEY SAY
ARE THE BEST
FOR KISSING.

*Dorothy Parker*

Love does not claim
possession, but
gives freedom.

*Rabindranath Tagore*

A kiss is a lovely trick
designed by nature to
stop speech when words
become superfluous.

INGRID
BERGMAN

Never love anyone
who treats you like
you're ordinary.

OSCAR WILDE

There is only one
happiness in this life,
to love and be loved.

GEORGE SAND

The good life is one
inspired by love and guided
by knowledge.

*Bertrand Russell*

THERE IS NO
LOVE WITHOUT
FORGIVENESS,
AND THERE IS NO
FORGIVENESS
WITHOUT LOVE.

*Bryant H. McGill*

THE MORE ONE
JUDGES, THE LESS
ONE LOVES.

*Honoré de Balzac*

Love doesn't make the
world go 'round. Love
is what makes the ride
worthwhile.

*Franklin P. Jones*

THE BEST AND MOST
beautiful things in the
world cannot be seen nor
even touched, but just
felt in the heart.

*Anne Sullivan*

THEY DO NOT LOVE
THAT DO NOT SHOW
THEIR LOVE.

*William Shakespeare*

YOU WILL NEVER
KNOW LOVE UNLESS
YOU SURRENDER
TO IT.

*Katherine Reback,*
Fools Rush In

Life without love is
like a tree without
blossoms or fruit.

*Khalil Gibran*

The most precious gift we can offer anyone is our attention. When mindfulness embraces those we love, they will bloom like flowers.

*Thich Nhat Hanh*

Some women choose to follow men, and some women choose to follow their dreams. If you're wondering which way to go, remember that your career will never wake up and tell you that it doesn't love you anymore.

*Lady Gaga*

WHAT'S MEANT TO BE WILL ALWAYS FIND A WAY.

*Trisha Yearwood*

Go after her. Fuck, don't sit there and wait for her to call, go after her because that's what you should do if you love someone, don't wait for them to give you a sign cause it might never come. . . . There are people I might have loved had they gotten on the airplane or run down the street after me or called me up drunk at four in the morning because they need to tell me right now. . . . Go scream it and be with her in meaningful ways because that is beautiful and that is generous and that is what loving someone is, that is raw and that is unguarded, and that is all that is worth anything, really.

HARVEY MILK

"Hey, Zaheera, I like you.
Will you be my girlfriend?"
Ten words that might have
changed my life if I'd had
the courage to say them.
But I hadn't, and now
she was gone.

TREVOR NOAH

THE ONE YOU LOVE
AND THE ONE WHO
LOVES YOU ARE
NEVER, EVER THE
SAME PERSON.

*Chuck Palahniuk*

You can't measure the
mutual affection of two
human beings by the
number of words they
exchange.

*Milan Kundera*

The beginning of love is
the will to let those we love
be perfectly themselves,
the resolution not to twist
them to fit our own image.

*Thomas Merton*

It is better to be hated for
what you are than to be
loved for what you are not.

*André Gide*

You learn to like someone
when you find out what
makes them laugh, but
you can never truly love
someone until you find out
what makes them cry.

*Unknown*

ONLY DO WHAT YOUR
HEART TELLS YOU.

*Princess Diana*

Love is like quicksilver
in the hand.

Leave the fingers open
and it stays.

Clutch it and it darts away.

DOROTHY
PARKER

Be careful of love. It'll twist
your brain around and
leave you thinking up is
down and right is wrong.

*Rick Riordan*

IN DREAMS AND IN
LOVE THERE ARE NO
IMPOSSIBILITIES.

*János Arany*

Have enough courage to
trust love one more time
and always one more time.

*Maya Angelou*

. . . the light you can see by.

*Bess Streeter Aldrich*

. . . the poetry of the senses.

*Honoré de Balzac*

. . . not what the mind thinks, but
what the heart feels.

*Greg Evans*

. . . a promise, love is a souvenir.
Once given, never forgotten.

*John Lennon*

. . . when he gives you a piece of your
soul, that you never knew was missing.

*Torquato Tasso*

When you are in love
with someone you want
to be near him all the
time, except when you are
buying things and charging
them to him.

MISS PIGGY

I'm selfish, impatient and a little insecure.
I make mistakes, I am out of control and
at times hard to handle. But if you can't
handle me at my worst, then you sure as
hell don't deserve me at my best.

MARILYN
MONROE

It is easy to love people in
memory; the hard thing
is to love them when they
are there in front of you.

*John Updike*

## THE BEST THING TO
## HOLD ONTO IN LIFE IS
## EACH OTHER.

*Audrey Hepburn*

## IT IS AN EXTRA
## DIVIDEND WHEN
## YOU LIKE THE GIRL
## YOU'VE FALLEN IN
## LOVE WITH.

*Clark Gable*

Love does not begin and
end the way we seem
to think it does. Love is
a battle, love is a war;
love is a growing up.

*James Baldwin*

It is not in the stars
to hold our destiny
but in ourselves.

WILLIAM
SHAKESPEARE

And now these three remain: faith, hope, and love. But the greatest of these is love.

*THE BIBLE*,
1 Corinthians
13:13

LOVE OBSERVED

There are only four questions
of value in life;

What is sacred, of what is the spirit
made, what is worth living for,
and what is worth dying for?

The answer to each is the same;
Only love.

DON JUAN
DEMARCO

LOVE IS A GREAT
BEAUTIFIER.

*Louisa May Alcott*

It's useless to hold a
person to anything he says
while he's in love, drunk,
or running for office.

*Shirley MacLaine*

Love can make even nice
people do awful things.

*Jude Deveraux*

Love is the state in which
a man sees things most
decidedly as what they are
not. The force of illusion
reaches its zenith here. . . .
When a man is in love
he endures more than
at other times. . . .

*Friedrich Nietzsche*

IN THE ARITHMETIC
OF LOVE, ONE
PLUS ONE EQUALS
EVERYTHING, AND
TWO MINUS ONE
EQUALS NOTHING.

*Mignon McLaughlin*

EVER HAS IT BEEN
THAT LOVE KNOWS
NOT ITS OWN DEPTH
UNTIL THE HOUR OF
SEPARATION.

*Kahlil Gibran*

When we are in love
we seem to ourselves quite
different from what we
were before.

*Blaise Pascal*

Our chief want in life is
somebody who shall make
us do what we can.

RALPH WALDO
EMERSON

The perfect lover is
one who turns into
a pizza at 4:00 a.m.

*Charles Pierce*

ONE MAN'S FOLLY IS
ANOTHER MAN'S WIFE.

*Helen Rowland*

*LOVE* IS THE SAME
AS *LIKE* EXCEPT YOU
FEEL SEXIER.

*Judith Viorst*

A man is already halfway
in love with any woman
who listens to him.

*Brendan Francis*

The wounds invisible
That loves keen
arrows make.

*William Shakespeare*

A lady's imagination
is very rapid; it jumps
from admiration to love,
from love to matrimony
in a moment.

*Jane Austen*

LOVE IN ITS ESSENCE
IS SPIRITUAL FIRE.

*Lucius Annaeus Seneca*

The greatest tragedy
of life is not that men
perish, but that they
cease to love.

*Somerset Maugham*

In love the paradox occurs
that two beings become
one and yet remain two.

*Erich Fromm*

THE ONLY REGRET I
WILL HAVE IN DYING IS
IF IT IS NOT FOR LOVE.

*Gabriel García Márquez*

LOVE MAKES
YOUR SOUL CRAWL
OUT FROM ITS
HIDING PLACE.

*Zora Neale Hurston*

The minute I heard my
first love story, I started
looking for you, not
knowing how blind that
was. Lovers don't finally
meet somewhere. They're
in each other all along.

*Rumi*

A woman with romance in
her life lived as grandly as
a queen, because her heart
was treasured.

*Nora Roberts*

The happiest liaisons
are based on mutual
misunderstanding.

FRANÇOIS
DE LA
ROCHEFOUCAULD

You can't stop loving or wanting to love because when it's right, it's the best thing in the world. When you're in a relationship and it's good, even if nothing else in your life is right, you feel like your whole world is complete.

KEITH SWEAT

TWO SOULS WITH BUT
A SINGLE THOUGHT,
TWO HEARTS THAT
BEAT AS ONE.

*John Keats*

Pure love is a willingness
to give without a thought
of receiving anything
in return.

*Peace Pilgrim*

Perhaps love is the process
of my gently leading
you back to yourself.

*Antoine de Saint-Exupéry*

WHAT IS HELL? I
MAINTAIN THAT IT
IS THE SUFFERING
OF BEING UNABLE
TO LOVE.

*Fyodor Dostoyevsky*

There is no feeling more
comforting and consoling
than knowing you are right
next to the one you love.

*Oscar Wilde*

THE PLEASURE OF
LOVE IS IN LOVING.
WE ARE HAPPIER IN
THE PASSION WE FEEL
THAN IN THAT
WE AROUSE.

*François de La Rochefoucauld*

Let no one who loves be
called unhappy. Even love
unreturned has its rainbow.

*J. M. Barrie*

Piglet: "How do you spell 'love'?"

Pooh: "You don't spell it. . . you feel it."

A. A. MILNE

There is a single magic,
a single power, a single
salvation, and a single
happiness, and that
is called loving.

HERMAN HESSE

. . . a game that two can play and
both win.

*Eva Gabor*

. . . the only game that is not called on
account of darkness.

*Thomas Carlyle*

. . . the only gold.

*Alfred Lord Tennyson*

. . . above all, the gift of oneself.

*Jean Anouilh*

. . . to love someone for who they are,
who they were, and who they will be.

*Chris Moore*

LOVE, AND A COUGH,
CANNOT BE HID.

*George Herbert*

Love recognizes no
barriers. It jumps hurdles,
leaps fences, penetrates
walls to arrive at its
destination full of hope.

*Maya Angelou*

Love has no limits. Love
never ends. Love is reborn
and reborn and reborn.

*Thich Nhat Hanh*

In their first passion women
love their lovers, in the
others they love love.

*François de La Rochefoucauld*

I love that feeling of being
in love, the effect of having
butterflies when you wake
up in the morning.

*Jennifer Aniston*

MY WISH IS THAT
YOU MAY BE LOVED
TO THE POINT OF
MADNESS.

*André Breton*

LOVE CREATES
AN "US" WITHOUT
DESTROYING
THE "ME."

*Leo Buscaglia*

Why can't love be simple?
Why can't it just be as pure
as two people who realize
that they can't live as well,
or as happily, apart as they
can together?

*Bella Andre*

FOR GOD SAKE HOLD
YOUR TONGUE,
AND LET ME LOVE.

*John Donne*

I love people who make me laugh. I honestly think it's the thing I like most, to laugh. It cures a multitude of ills. It's probably the most important thing in a person.

AUDREY
HEPBURN

A woman without a man
cannot meet a man,
any man, of any age,
without thinking, even
if it's for a half-second,
*Perhaps this is the man.*

DORIS LESSING

In my sex fantasy, nobody
ever loves me for my mind.

*Nora Ephron*

I NEED SEX FOR A
CLEAR COMPLEXION,
BUT I'D RATHER DO IT
FOR LOVE.

*Joan Crawford*

WOMEN NEED A
REASON TO HAVE SEX.
MEN JUST NEED
A PLACE.

*Billy Crystal*

THE BEST PROOF OF
LOVE IS TRUST.

*Joyce Brothers*

One is loved because
one is loved. No reason
is needed for loving.

*Paulo Coelho*

If only one could tell true
love from false love as one
can tell mushrooms
from toadstools.

*Katherine Mansfield*

LOVE IS LIKE A VIRUS.
IT CAN HAPPEN
TO ANYBODY AT
ANY TIME.

*Maya Angelou*

What is irritating about
love is that it is a crime that
requires an accomplice.

*Charles Baudelaire*

MAGIC EXISTS. . . .
ANYONE WHO HAS
LOVED HAS BEEN
TOUCHED BY MAGIC.

*Nora Roberts*

WE ARE SHAPED
AND FASHIONED BY
THOSE WE LOVE.

*Goethe*

A MAN IN LOVE
MISTAKES A PIMPLE
FOR A DIMPLE.

*Japanese proverb*

The highest function of
love is that it makes the
loved one a unique and
irreplaceable being.

*Tom Robbins*

To love is nothing. To be
loved is something. But to
love and be loved, that's
everything.

*T. Tolis*

Many a man in love with a
dimple makes a mistake of
marrying the whole girl.

*Stephen Leacock*

ANYONE CAN BE
PASSIONATE, BUT IT
TAKES REAL LOVERS
TO BE SILLY.

*Rose Franken*

Love is like an hourglass,
with the heart filling up
as the brain empties.

*Jules Renard*

LOVE LIBERATES. IT
DOESN'T BIND.

*Maya Angelou*

Who can give law
to lovers?

Love is a greater law
to itself.

BOETHIUS

The human race has been set up. Someone, somewhere, is playing a practical joke on us. Apparently, women need to feel loved to have sex. Men need to have sex to feel loved. How do we ever get started?

BILLY CONNOLLY

The only thing worse
than a boy who hates you:
a boy that loves you.

MARKUS ZUSAK

I think. . . if it is true that
there are as many minds as there
are heads, then there are as many
kinds of love as there are hearts.

LEO TOLSTOY

# COUNTRY-WESTERN LOVE SONGS

How Can I Miss You If You Won't Go Away?

•

## I Changed Her Oil, She Changed My Life

•

I Fell In A Pile Of You And Got Love All Over Me

•

## If You Leave Me, Can I Come Too?

•

My Wife Ran Off With My Best Friend,
And I Sure Do Miss Him

•

## Velcro Arms, Teflon Heart

•

You Done Tore Out My Heart And Stomped
That Sucker Flat

•

## I Married Her Just Because She Looks Like You

I Can't Love Your Body If Your Heart's Not In It

•

I'm So Miserable Without You It's Like Having You Here

•

I Keep Forgettin' I Forgot About You

•

If You Don't Believe I Love You Just Ask My Wife

•

The Worst You Ever Gave Me Was the Best I Ever Had

•

We Used to Just Kiss on the Lips But Now It's All Over

•

It Don't Hurt Half as Bad as Holding You Feels Good

•

I Liked You Better Before I Knew You So Well

•

If Love Were Oil, I'd Be A Quart Low

## PARADISE IS ALWAYS
## WHERE LOVE DWELLS.

*Jean Paul Richter*

In our life there is a single
color, as on an artist's
palette, which provides the
meaning of life and art.
It is the color of love.

*Marc Chagall*

Love can change a person
the way a parent can
change a baby—awkwardly,
and often with a great
deal of mess.

*Lemony Snicket*

Words may be false
and full of art;
Sighs are the natural
language of the heart.

*Thomas Shadwell*

Love lets you find those hidden places
in another person, even the ones they
didn't know were there, even the ones
they wouldn't have thought to call
beautiful themselves.

HILARY T. SMITH

ABSENCE MAKES
THE HEART GROW
FONDER.

*Unknown*

They say absence makes
the heart grow fonder,
so I figure that's why my
boyfriend moved.

*Christy Murphy*

TO LOVE IS TO
RECEIVE A GLIMPSE
OF HEAVEN.

*Karen Sunde*

It isn't possible to love and
part. You will wish that it
was. You can transmute
love, ignore it, muddle
it, but you can never pull
it out of you. I know by
experience that the poets
are right: love is eternal.

*E.M. Forster*

MAY YOU LIVE AS
LONG AS YOU WISH
AND LOVE AS LONG
AS YOU LIVE.

*Robert A. Heinlein*

I am nothing special, of this I am sure.
I am a common man with common thoughts
and I've led a common life. There are
no monuments dedicated to me and my
name will soon be forgotten, but I've loved
another with all my heart and soul, and to
me, this has always been enough.

NICHOLAS
SPARKS

SOMETIMES THE
HEART SEES WHAT IS
INVISIBLE TO THE EYE.

*H. Jackson Brown Jr.*

Of all the earthly music,
that which reaches farthest
into heaven is the beating
of a truly loving heart.

*Henry Ward Beecher*

The madness of love
is the greatest of
heaven's blessings.

*Plato*

THE ESSENCE OF
LOVE IS CREATIVE
COMPANIONSHIP, THE
FULFILLMENT OF ONE
LIFE BY ANOTHER.

*John Erskine*

If I know what love is,
it is because of you.

HERMAN HESSE

Being deeply loved by someone gives you strength, while loving someone deeply gives you courage.

LAO-TZU

Love is said to be blind,
but I know lots of fellows in
love who can see
twice as much in their
sweethearts as I can.

*Josh Billings*

THE MOST HAPPY
MARRIAGE I CAN
IMAGINE TO MYSELF
WOULD BE THE
UNION OF A DEAF
MAN TO A BLIND
WOMAN.

*Samuel Taylor Coleridge*

Love is blind they say,
but isn't it more that love
makes us see too much?
Isn't it more that love
floods our brain with sights
and sounds, so that
everything looks bigger,
brighter, more lovely than
ever before?

*Susan Fletcher*

PEOPLE WHO
THROW KISSES ARE
HOPELESSLY LAZY.

*Bob Hope*

There is no feeling in a
human heart which exists
in that heart alone—which
is not, in some form or
degree, in every heart.

*George Macdonald*

A man does not find
his heart until he has lost
his head.

*Friedrich Nietzsche*

. . . much like a wild rose, beautiful
and calm, but willing to draw blood
in its defense.

*Mark Overby*

. . . an exploding cigar we willingly
smoke.

*Lynda Barry*

. . . of all passions the strongest, for it
attacks simultaneously the head, the
heart, and the senses.

*Lao Tzu*

. . . friendship set on fire.

*Jeremy Taylor*

. . . a very dangerous state. I don't know
who the hell wants to get in
a situation where you can't bear an hour
without somebody's company.

*Colin Firth*

A LOVING HEART IS
THE TRUEST WISDOM.

*Charles Dickens*

In the coldest February,
as in every month in every
other year, the best thing
we can hold onto
is each other.

*Linda Ellerbee*

Nobody has ever
measured, not even
poets, how much
the heart can hold.

*Zelda Fitzgerald*

TWO PEOPLE IN LOVE,
ALONE, ISOLATED
FROM THE WORLD,
THAT'S BEAUTIFUL.

*Milan Kundera*

*The Velveteen Rabbit*

Generally, by the time you are
Real, most of your hair has been
loved off, and your eyes drop out
and you get loose in the joints and
very shabby. But these things don't
matter at all, because once you are
Real you can't be ugly, except to
people who don't understand.

MARGERY
WILLIAMS

LOVE BEYOND

I don't want the heavens or the shooting stars. I don't want gemstones or gold. I have those things already. I want a steady hand, a kind soul. I want to fall asleep and wake knowing my heart is safe. I want to love and be loved.

SHANA ABE

When you realize you want to spend the rest of your life with somebody, you want the rest of your life to start as soon as possible.

NORA EPHRON

## LOVE IS OFTEN THE FRUIT OF MARRIAGE.

*Molière*

Marriage is like a besieged fortress. Everyone outside wants to get in, and everyone inside wants to get out.

*French proverb*

The most wonderful thing about marriage is that you are the most important person in someone else's life. If you don't come home some evening, there is someone who is going to go out looking for you.

*Joyce Brothers*

I love being married. . . . It's so great to find that one special person you want to annoy for the rest of your life.

*Rita Rudner*

All men make mistakes,
but married men find out
about them sooner.

RED SKELTON

One good reason to get married is you'll always have someone to blame when you can't find your keys.

JOHN LOUIS
ANDERSON

I WONDER WHAT
ADAM AND EVE THINK
OF IT BY THIS TIME.

*Marianne Moore*

This is a good sign, having
a broken heart. It means we
have tried for something.

*Elizabeth Gilbert*

When two people are
under the influence of
the most violent, most
insane, most delusive, and
most transient of passions,
they are required to swear
that they will remain in
that excited, abnormal,
and exhausting condition
continuously until death
do them part.

*George Bernard Shaw*

Close the door when you
get home from work, and
hug and kiss with someone
special for at least fifteen
minutes—longer is better.

*Anita Baker*

Marriage is based on
the theory that when a man
discovers a brand of beer
exactly to his taste
he should at once throw
up his job and go to work
in the brewery.

*George Jean Nathan*

A GOOD MARRIAGE
IS LIKE A CASSEROLE,
ONLY THOSE
RESPONSIBLE FOR IT
REALLY KNOW WHAT
GOES INTO IT.

*Unknown*

You know, when it works,
love is pretty amazing.

It's not overrated. There's a
reason for all those songs.

SARAH DESSEN

If it weren't for marriage,
men and women would
have to fight with
total strangers.

*Unknown*

Trouble is part of life—
if you don't share it, you
don't give the person who
loves you a chance to
love you enough.

*Dinah Shore*

When we lose one we love,
our bitterest tears
are called forth by the
memory of hours when
we loved not enough.

*Maurice Maeterlinck*

Love lasts about seven years. That's how long it takes for the cells of the body to totally replace themselves.

*Françoise Sagan*

GROW OLD WITH ME!
THE BEST IS YET
TO BE.

*Robert Browning*

Love at first sight is easy to understand; it's when two people have been looking at each other for a lifetime that it becomes a miracle.

*Sam Levenson*

LOVE HAS NO AGE,
AS IT IS ALWAYS
RENEWING.

*Blaise Pascal*

Well, it seems to me that the best relationships—the ones that last—are frequently the ones that are rooted in friendship. You know, one day you look at the person and you see something more than you did the night before. Like a switch has been flicked somewhere. And the person who was just a friend is. . . suddenly the only person you can ever imagine yourself with.

GILLIAN
ANDERSON

Men always want to be
a woman's first love—
women like to be a man's
last romance.

*Oscar Wilde*

And ever has it been
known that love knows
not its own depth until the
hour of separation.

*Khalil Gibran*

THE FIRST TIME YOU
MARRY FOR LOVE, THE
SECOND FOR MONEY,
AND THE THIRD FOR
COMPANIONSHIP.

*Jackie Kennedy*

Sometimes it was worth
all the disadvantages of
marriage just to have that:
One friend in an
indifferent world.

*Erica Jong*

The best part of married
life is the fights. The rest is
merely so-so.

*Thornton Wilder*

MARRIAGE IS A GREAT
INSTITUTION, BUT
I'M NOT READY FOR
AN INSTITUTION.

*Mae West*

The best thing that can
happen to a couple married
for fifty years or more
is that they both grow
nearsighted together.

*Linda Fiterman*

Love grows more
tremendously full,
swift, poignant, as the
years multiply.

*Zane Grey*

What scares me about divorce is that my children might put me in a home for unwed mothers.

TERESSA
SKELTON

How do you know love is gone?
If you said that you would be there
at seven and you get there by
nine, and he or she has not called
the police—it's gone.

MARLENE
DIETRICH

Love never dies a natural death.
It dies because we don't know how to
replenish its source. It dies of blindness
and errors and betrayals. It dies of illness
and wounds; it dies of weariness,
of witherings, of tarnishings.

ANAÏS NIN

YOU CAN'T BUY LOVE,
BUT YOU CAN PAY
HEAVILY FOR IT.

*Henny Youngman*

My boyfriend and I
broke up. He wanted to
get married and I didn't
want him to.

*Rita Rudner*

It's the clichés that cause the trouble.
To lose someone you love is to alter your
life for ever. You don't get over it because
"it" is the person you loved. The pain stops,
there are new people, but the gap never
closes. How could it? The particularness
of someone who mattered enough to
grieve over is not made anodyne by death.
This hole in my heart is in the shape
of you and no-one else can fit it.
Why would I want them to?

JEANETTE
WINTERSON

ONE REASON PEOPLE
GET DIVORCED IS
THAT THEY RUN OUT
OF GIFT IDEAS.

*Robert Byrne*

A divorce is like an
amputation: you survive it,
but there's less of you.

*Margaret Atwood*

PLEASURE OF
LOVE LASTS BUT
A MOMENT. PAIN
OF LOVE LASTS
A LIFETIME.

*Bette Davis*

Looking back,
I have this to regret,
that too often when I loved,
I did not say so.

DAVID GRAYSON

But to see her was to love her,

Love but her, and love forever.

Had we never lov'd sae kindly,

Had we never lov'd sae blindly,

Never met—or never parted—

We had ne'er been brokenhearted.

ROBERT BURNS

There is only one page left
to write on.
I will fill it with words of only
one syllable.

I love. I have loved. I will love.

AUDREY
NIFFENEGGER

Designer: Hana Anouk Nakamura
Custom Typography by Nick Misani
ISBN: 978-1-4197-3263-8
Foreword © 2018 Bella Andre
© 2018 Abrams Noterie

Printed and bound in China
10 9 8 7 6 5 4 3 2 1

**ABRAMS** The Art of Books
195 Broadway, New York, NY 10007
abramsbooks.com